CARL MARIA VON WEBER

EURYANTHE

Overture to the Opera
Op. 81

Ernst Eulenburg Ltd
London · Mainz · New York · Tokyo · Zürich

Euryanthe

Overture

C. M. von Weber, Op. 81
1786 - 1826

Allegro marcato, con molto fuoco. 𝅗𝅥 = 92.

2 Flauti
2 Oboi
2 Clarinetti in B
2 Fagotti
4 Corni I. II. in B
III. IV. in Es
2 Trombe in Es
Tromboni Alto
Tenore
Basso
Timpani in Es-B
Violino I
Violino II
Viola
Violoncello
Contrabasso

ff

EE 3735

Ernst Eulenburg Ltd

Fl.
Ob.
Cl.
Fg.
(B)
Cor.
(Es)
Tbe.
(Es)
Tbni.
Timp.
Vl.
Vla.
Vc.
Cb.
ff

10
Fl.
Ob
Cl.
Fg.
(B)
Cor.
(Es)
Tbe.
(Es)
Tbni.
Timp.
Vl.
Vla.
Vc.
Cb.
ff

Fl.
Ob.
Cl.
Fg.
(B)
Cor.
(Es)
Tbe.
(Es)
mf
Tbni.
Timp.
mf
Vl.
Vla.
Vc.
Cb.

20
I.
Fl.
Ob.
Cl.
Fg.
(B)
Cor.
(Es)
Tbe.
(Es)
Tbni.
Timp.
Vl.
Vla.
Vc.
Cb.
p
p
ff
ff
ff
ff
ff

80
Fl.
Ob.
Cl.
Fg.
(B)
Cor.
(Es)
Tbe.
(Es)
Tbni.
Timp.
Vl.
Vla.
Vc.
Cb.
ff
f
6

Fl.
Ob.
Cl.
Fg
(B)
Cor.
(Es)
Tbe.
(Es)
Tbni.
Timp.
Vl.
Vla.
Vc.
Cb.

Fl.
Ob.
Cl.
Fg.
a 2
Cor. (Es)
3.4.
Tbe. (Es)
Timp.
Vl.
Vla.
Vc. Cb.
40

Fl.
Ob.
Cl.
Fg.
(B)
Cor.
(Es)
Tbe.
(Es)
Tbni.
Timp.
Vl.
Vla.
Vc.
Cb.
a 2.
a 2.

50
Fl.
Ob.
Cl.
Fg.
(B)
Cor.
(Es)
Tbe.
(Es)
Tbni.
Timp.
Vl
Vla.
Vc.
Cb.
ff

Fl.
Ob.
à 2.
ff
Cl.
Fg.
(B)
Cor.
(Es)
Tbe.
(Es)
Tbni.
Timp.
3
Vl.
Vla.
p
Vc.
dolce
Cb.

60
dolce
Vl.
Vla.
Vc.
Cb.
Cl.
Fg.
pp
pp
Vl.
Vla.
Vc.
Cb.

Cl.
Fg.
3.4.
Cor. Es)
mf
Vl.
Vla.
Vc.
Cb.
80
Fg.
Vl.
Vla.
Vc.
Cb.

Fl.
Ob.
Cl.
Fg.
(B)
Cor.
(Es)
Tbe.
(Es)
Tbni.
Timp.
Vl.
Vla.
Vc.
Cb.
ff
3

90
Fl.
Ob.
Cl.
Fg.
(B)
Cor.
(Es)
Tbe.
(Es)
Tbni.
Timp.
Vl.
Vla.
Vc.
Cb.
ff
3

Fl.
Ob.
Cl.
Fg.
(B)
Cor.
Es)
Tbe.
(Es)
Tbni.
Timp.
Vl.
Vla.
Vc.
Cb.
ff

100
Fl.
Ob
Cl
Fg.
(B)
Cor.
(Es)
Tbe.
(Es)
Tbni.
Timp.
Vl.
Vla.
Vc.
Cb.
ff
3

Fl.
Ob.
Cl.
Fg.
(B)
Cor.
(Es)
Tbe.
(Es)
Tbni.
Timp.
Vl.
Vla.
Vc.
Cb.
sempre fortissimo
sempre fortissimo
ff

110
Fl.
Ob.
Cl.
Fg.
(B)
Cor.
(Es)
Tbe.
(Es)
Tbni.
Timp.
Vl.
Vla.
Vc.
Cb.
p
pp

Cl.
Fg.
Cor.
(Es)
3.4.
Solo
Vl.
pp
Vla.
Vc.
Fg.
Cor.
(Es)
Tenore
Tbni.
Basso
pp
Timp.
pp
Vl.I
pp
Vla.
pp

Largo. 𝅗𝅥 = 52
130
8 Violinen con Sordino
pp
Vla.
140
ppp
8 Vl.
Vla.
Vc.
Cb.
Tempo I assai moderato. 𝅗𝅥 = 88
senza sordini
Vl. II
Vla.
Vc.
Cb.
3

150
Vl.
Vla.
Vc.
Cb.
mf
Fg.
Tbne.
pp
f
p
160
ff

Ob.
Cl.
Fg.
(B)
Cor.
(Es)
Tbne.
Vl.
Vla.
Vc.
Cb.
unis.
Fl.
170

Fl.
Ob
Cl
ff
Fg.
ff
(B)
Cor.
(Es)
ff
Tbe.
(Es)
ff
Tbni.
ff
ff
ff
Timp.
ff
Vl.
Vla.
Vc.
Cb.

Fl.
Ob.
Cl.
Fg.
(B)
Cor.
(Es)
Tbe.
(Es)
Tbni.
Timp.
Vl.
Vla.
Vc.
Cb.
ff
cresc.

180
Fl.
Ob.
Cl
Fg.
(B)
Cor.
(Es)
Tbe.
(Es)
Tbni.
Timp.
Vl
Vla.
Vc.
Cb.

stringendo
poco
a
poco
Fl.
Ob.
a 2.
ff
Cl
ff
Fg.
(B)
Cor.
(Es)
ff
ff
Tbe.
(Es)
Tbni.
Timp.
Vl.
Vla.
Vc.
ff
Cb.
ff

Tempo I. 190

Fl.

Ob.

Cl.

Fg.

(B)
Cor.
(Es)

Tbe.
(Es)

Tbni.

Timp.

Vl.

Vla.

Vc.

Cb.

ff

Fl.
Ob.
Cl.
Fg.
(B)
Cor.
(Es)
Tbe.
(Es)
Tbni.
Timp.
Vl.
Vla.
Vc.
Cb.
pp
p

Fl.
Ob.
Cl.
Fg
(B)
Cor.
(Es)
Tbe.
(Es)
Tbni.
Timp.
Vl.
Vla.
Vc.
Cb.
à 2.
à 2.
ff

200
Fl.
Ob.
Cl.
Fg.
(B)
Cor.
(Es)
Tbe.
(Es)
Tbni.
Timp.
Vl.
Vla.
Vc.
Cb.
ff

a 2
Fl.
Ob.
Cl.
Fg.
(B)
Cor.
(Es)
Tbe.
(Es)
Tbni.
Timp.
Vl.
Vla.
Vc.
Cb.

210
Fl.
Ob.
Cl.
Fg.
(B)
Cor.
(Es)
Tbe.
(Es)
Tbni.
Timp.
Vl.
Vla.
Vc.
Cb.
ff

Fl.
Ob.
Cl.
Fg.
a 2
3.4.
Cor. (Es)
Tbe. (Es)
Timp.
Vl.
Vla.
Vc. Cb.

Fl.
Ob.
Cl.
Fg.
Vl.
Vla.
Vc. Cb.

220
Fl.
Ob.
Cl.
Fg
(B)
Cor.
(Es)
Tbe.
(Es)
Tbni.
Timp.
Vl.
Vla.
Vc.
Cb.
ff

Fl.
Ob.
Cl
Fg
(B)
Cor.
(Es)
Tbe.
(Es)
Tbni.
Timp
Vl.
Vla.
Vc.
Cb.
ff
f

230
Fl.
Ob.
Cl.
à 2.
Fg.
(B)
Cor.
(Es)
Tbe.
(Es)
Tbni.
Timp.
Vl.
Vla.
Vc.
Cb.
ff

240
Fl.
Ob.
Cl.
Fg.
(B)
Cor.
(Es)
Tbe.
(Es)
ff
Tbni.
Timp.
ff
Vl.
Vla.
Vc.
Cb.

Fl.
Ob.
Cl.
Fg.
(B)
Cor.
(Es)
Tbe.
(Es)
Tbni.
Timp.
p
Vl.
Vla.
Vc.
Cb.

Fl.
Ob.
Cl.
Fg.
à 2.
(B)
Cor.
(Es)
Tbe.
(Es)
Tbni.
f
f
f
Timp.
ff
Vl.
Vla.
Vc.
Cb.

250
Fl.
Ob.
Cl.
Fg.
(B)
Cor.
(Es)
Tbe.
(Es)
Tbni
Timp.
Vl.
Vla.
Vc.
Cb.
ff

Fl.
Ob.
Cl.
Fg.
(B)
Cor.
(Es)
Tbe.
(Es)
Tbni.
Timp.
Vl.
Vla.
Vc
Cb.

260
Fl.
Ob.
Cl.
Fg.
(B)
Cor.
(Es)
Tbe.
(Es)
Tbni.
Timp.
Vl.
Vla.
Vc.
Cb.
ff

Fl.
Ob.
Cl
Fg.
(B)
Cor.
(Es)
Tbe.
(Es)
Tbni.
Timp.
Vl.
Vla.
Vc.
Cb.
ff
ff
ff
ff

270
a 2.
a 2.
Fl.
ff
Ob.
Cl.
Fg.
(B)
Cor.
(Es)
Tbe.
(Es)
ff
ff
ff
bni.
ff
Timp.
ff
Vl.
Vla.
Vc.
Cb.

Fl.
Ob.
Cl.
Fg.
(B)
Cor.
(Es)
Tbe.
(Es)
Tbni.
Timp.
Vl.
Vla.
Vc.
Cb.
ff
6